Copycat Recipes

Made Easy

A Simply Cookbook on How to Make the Most

Popular Restaurant Dishes Directly to Your Home

Ginger Bennet

Disclaimer Notice:

Please note the information contained within this document is for educational and entertainment purposes only. All effort has been executed to present accurate, up to date, and reliable, complete information. No warranties of any kind are declared or implied. Readers acknowledge that the author is not engaging in the rendering of legal, financial, medical or professional advice. The content within this book has been derived from various sources. Please consult a licensed professional before attempting any techniques outlined in this book.

By reading this document, the reader agrees that under no circumstances is the author responsible for any losses, direct or indirect, which are incurred as a result of the use of information contained within this document, including, but not limited to, errors, omissions, or inaccuracies.

Table Of Content

Introduction

Thank You For Purchasing **Copycat Recipes Made Easy: A Simply Cookbook on How to Make the Most Popular Restaurant Dishes Directly to Your Home**

Some people think that a degree in culinary is needed to be able to create secret recipes. The truth is that anyone can collect the ingredients themselves and cook a meal that tastes just like restaurant food.

Sooner or later, there is a need that every person cooks their own food. Of course, lately, fast-food restaurants have been growing like mushrooms, and the freezers of all stores are littered with semi-finished products, but that doesn't solve the problem. Firstly, it's quite expensive, secondly, most often it's tasteless and, thirdly, it's certainly not useful.

Breakfast

Paris' Lyonnaise Potatoes

Preparation Time: 10 minutes

Cooking Time: 35 minutes

Servings: 4

Ingredients:

1.   2 pounds of russet potatoes (peeled, sliced in rounds of half an inch)

2.   3 tablespoons butter

3.   4 tablespoons vegetable oil

4.   2 onions (sliced thinly)

5.   ½ cup parsley (chopped)

6.   1 tablespoon kosher salt

Directions:

1.   Boil the potatoes in water in a large pot. Cook for four minutes until the potatoes are crisp tender. Drain the water.

2.   Take an iron skillet and heat one tablespoon butter in it. Add one tablespoon the vegetable oil. Put half of the onions and potatoes to the skillet. Cook the mixture for 5 minutes.

Add the remaining oil, butter, onions, and potatoes to the skillet. Cook for fifteen minutes until the onions are browned.

3.   Remove the skillet from heat and add parsley from the top. Serve with pepper and salt from the top.

Nutrition:

- Calories: 320

- Protein: 3.6g

- Carbs: 33g

- Fat: 19.2g

- Sugar: 4g

Paris' Cheddar and Dill Puffs

Preparation Time: 20 minutes

Cooking Time: 30 minutes

Servings: 20

Ingredients:

- 1 cup water

- ½ cup butter (unsalted)

- ½ tablespoon kosher salt

- 1 cup flour

- 5 large eggs

- 1 ½ cup cheddar cheese (grated)

- 2 tablespoons fresh dill (chopped)

Directions:

1.   Preheat oven at 180°C.

2.   Take a saucepan and heat it over a medium flame. Add butter, water, and salt to the pan. Simmer the mixture and keep cooking until the butter melts. Mix the flour to the pan and stir continuously. Cook for two minutes.

3.   Add the eggs to the batter. The mixture needs to be glossy and stiff enough for holding the peaks. In case the batter gets too stiff, you can add more eggs to the batter. Add the dill and cheese. Use parchment paper for lining two baking sheets. Use a scoop for dropping the batter on the trays. Bake the puffs until crispy and golden in color for thirty minutes.

Nutrition:

- Calories: 103
- Protein: 5g
- Carbs: 5.2g
- Fat: 6.8g
- Sugar: 1.1g

Cracker Barrel's Apple-Cheddar Chicken

Preparation Time: 10 minutes

Cooking Time: 45 minutes

Servings: 4–6

Ingredients:

- 5 cooked skinless hen breasts, entire or cubed

- 2 cans of apple pie filling with a cut of apples in ⅓

- 1 bag extra-sharp cheddar cheese

- 1 row Ritz crackers, beaten

- 1 cup melted butter

Directions:

1.   Preheat the oven to 350°F. Combine the chicken, apple pie filling, and cheddar cheese in a mixing bowl. Stir together. Pour the mixture in the casserole dish that has been greased.

2.   Mix the Ritz crackers with the melted butter. Spread over the casserole. Bake for 45 minutes or till it starts evolved to bubble.

Nutrition:

- Calories: 158

- Fat: 10g

- Carbs: 71g

- Protein: 7g

Paris' Salad Nicoise

Preparation Time: 10 minutes

Cooking Time: 20 minutes

Servings: 6

Ingredients:

- 8 ounces green beans (halved)
- 4 eggs
- 2 tablespoons each
- Red wine vinegar
- Dijon mustard
- ¼ cup olive oil (extra virgin)
- Black pepper (ground)
- Kosher salt
- 2 sliced romaine hearts
- 7 ounces canned tuna (drained)
- 2 cups cherry tomatoes (halved)
- 1 cup olives (sliced)

Directions:

1.   Boil a pan of water with salt on medium heat. Add the green beans and cook for one minute. Wash the beans under cold water and pat dry them using a paper towel.

2.   Again boil water in the pan and cook the eggs for ten minutes. Peel the boiled eggs and cut them lengthwise. Mix the mustard, oil, salt, pepper, and vinegar in a bowl. Add the sliced romaine for combining. Divide the salad among bowls and top it with tomatoes, tuna, green beans, olives, and sliced eggs.

Nutrition:

- Calories: 382.2

- Protein: 24g

- Carbs: 37.1g

- Fat: 17.8g

BJ Restaurant's Fresh Mozzarella and Tomato Salad

Preparation Time: 20 minutes

Cooking Time: 0 minutes

Servings: 4

Ingredients:

- 4 plum tomatoes, chopped

- 4 ounces fresh mozzarella cheese pearls, drained

- ¼ cup minced fresh basil

- ½ tablespoon minced fresh parsley

- 1 teaspoon minced fresh mint

- 2 tablespoons lemon juice

- 2 tablespoons olive oil

- ¼ teaspoon salt

- ⅛ Teaspoon black pepper

- 2 medium ripe avocados, peeled and chopped

Directions:

1. Prepare the veggies for the salad;

2. Take plum tomatoes and chop them;

3.   Transfer the tomatoes to a salad bowl;

4.   Spread a cheesecloth in a bowl and place the mozzarella cheese in this cheesecloth;

5.   Hold the cheese in the cheesecloth and squeeze it to drain all the liquid out;

6.   You can directly add the cheese pearls to the salad bowl or cut them in half to add to salad;

7.   Take the mint and parsley sprigs and remove the stem from the leaves;

8.   Chop the mint and parsley leaves then add to the salad bowl;

9.   Toss in basil and mix all the veggies and cheese pearls well;

10.   Refrigerate this salad for 15 minutes;

11.   Meanwhile, prepare the salad dressing;

12.   Take a small bowl, add lemon juice, black pepper, oil, and salt;

13.   Mix these ingredients well then pour this dressing over the tomato salad;

14.   Toss the salad again with the dressing to coat well;

15. Cover this mozzarella salad and refrigerate for 1 hour;

16. Cut the avocados in half and remove the pit;

17. Remove the avocado flesh and dice the flesh into cubes;

18. Add the avocado cubes to the tomato salad;

19. Serve fresh.

Nutrition:

- Calories: 178

- Fat: 15g

- Carbs: 50g

- Sugars: 8g

- Protein: 9g

Cracker Barrel's Corn Muffins

Preparation Time: 20 minutes

Cooking Time: 30 minutes

Servings: 12

Ingredients:

- ¾ cup yellow cornmeal

- 1¼ cups self-rising flour

- ½ cup sugar

- 2 massive eggs

- 2 tablespoons honey

- ¾ cup buttermilk

- ½ cup unsalted butter, melted and cooled

Directions:

1. Preheat the oven to 350°F.

2. Put a line in a muffin pan using muffin liner or grease thoroughly.

3. Combine the cornmeal, flour, and sugar in a mixing bowl.

4. Beat the eggs in a medium bowl. Then, add the honey and buttermilk and whisk till nicely combined.

5. Slowly add the buttermilk to the cornmeal mixture, stirring as you add. There are some lumps, but don't over-mix.

6. Place the batter inside the muffin pan and fill holes to the ¾, and bake for 18–20 minutes or until set.

7. Remove from oven and enable to cool barely earlier than serving.

Nutrition:

1. Calories: 184

2. Fat: 4g

3. Carbs: 57g

4. Protein: 12g

Main

Cracker Barrel's Meatloaf

Preparation Time: 10 minutes

Cooking Time: 1 hour and 10 minutes

Servings: 4

Ingredients:

- 1 pound ground beef

- 1 onion, chopped

- 1 green pepper, chopped

- 1 can chopped tomatoes

- 1 egg

- ½ cup frozen biscuits, shredded

- 1 teaspoon salt

- ¼ cup ketchup (optional)

- Non-stick cooking spray

Directions:

1. Preheat oven to 350°F.

2. In a bowl, add beef, onion, green pepper, tomatoes, egg, biscuits, and salt. Mix well.

3. Using a non-stick cooking spray, coat bread pan. Then, pour the meatloaf mixture into the pan. Make sure the mixture is even and flat in the pan.

4. Bake for 1 hour and 5 minutes. Let it cool for about 10 minutes.

5. Drain excess juice, then invert cooked meatloaf onto a serving plate. Drizzle ketchup on top, if desired. Serve.

Nutrition:

- Calories: 485

- Fat: 32g

- Carbs: 27g

- Protein: 23g

Maggiano's Little Italy's Beef Medallion

Preparation Time: 15 minutes

Cooking Time: 30 minutes

Servings: 4

Ingredients:

- ¾ cup dry wine

- 2 cups beef broth

- ¼ teaspoon of freshly ground black pepper

- ¾ cup whipping cream

- 2 tablespoons of mixed dried wild mushrooms

- 1 teaspoon of roasted garlic

- 2 teaspoons of canola oil

- Salt to taste

- ¼ cup diced shallots

- 8 beef medallions

- 1 tablespoon of softened butter

Directions:

1. Preheat your oven to 350°F.

2.   Let the mushrooms be soaked in warm water for 20 minutes or until soft. Strain and reserve the liquid to be used later.

3.   Heat one teaspoon of oil and the butter in a pan over medium heat, add shallots, mushrooms and roasted garlic, then cook until shallots start to brown, about 4 minutes, stirring frequently.

4.   Pour in the wine and after for 2–3 minutes, add the broth and allow to simmer until the mixture loses half its moisture, about 8 minutes.

5.   Rub the pepper and salt into the beef, heat the remaining oil into a large skillet over medium heat, then sear the meat for 2–3 minutes on each side.

6.   Put into the oven and cook for 10–20 minutes until tender.

7.   Serve it with some sauce on top.

Nutrition:

- Calories: 112

- Fat: 17g

- Carbs: 50g

- Sugars: 5g

- Protein: 7g

Sbarro's Chicken Francese

Preparation Time: 10 minutes

Cooking Time: 30 minutes

Servings: 8

Ingredients:

- 5 (5-ounces) chicken bosoms

- 5 eggs

- 3 ounces Romano cheddar

- 1 teaspoon of dehydrated parsley

- 1 cup flour

- Pinch white pepper

- 1 cup chicken stock

- ½ pound spread juice from 2 lemons

- 1.5 cups oil (10% olive oil, 90% vegetable oil)

Directions:

1. Lemon cuts and cleaved new parsley for embellish

Pound chicken bosoms level and cut down the middle.

2.   Put in a safe spot. Scramble eggs in the blending bowl. Include Romano cheddar, parsley, and white pepper. Blend and keep safe.

3.   Put flour in a huge shallow bowl.

4.   In a skillet, heat oil over medium warmth. Check the temperature by plunging an edge of a chicken piece in oil. On the off chance that it bubbles gradually, oil is prepared. Coat the two sides of a bit of chicken with flour. Dunk chicken in egg blend, ensuring all flour is secured with egg. Let abundance egg dribble off, at that point place chicken in hot oil. Rehash with 4 additional pieces. Fry each side of chicken until light fair shading. Expel from oil to a serving plate – keep warm. Rehash with other chicken pieces.

5.   Carry chicken stock to a light bubble. Include spread, mixing consistently, until liquefied. Include lemon squeeze and cook for 1 moment while mixing persistently. Pour sauce over chicken and enhancement with lemon cuts and slashed new parsley.

Nutrition:

•   Calories: 150

- Fat: 4.2g

- Carbs: 40g

- Sugars: 1g

- Protein: 9g

Maggiano's Little Italy's New York Steak Al Forno

Preparation Time: 20 minutes

Cooking Time: 15 minutes

Servings: 3

Ingredients:

- Salt and pepper to taste

- 1 New York steak (large)

- ¼ cup sliced gorgonzola cheese

- ½ cup sliced red onion

- 1 tablespoon chopped parsley and basil

- 1 tablespoon softened butter

- 1 tablespoon garlic butter

- ¼ cup balsamic sauce

- 3 ounces roasted portabella mushrooms

- Herb Marinade

- ¼ cup chopped fresh thyme leaves

- ½ cup olive oil

- ¼ cup minced garlic

- 1 tablespoon of freshly ground whole black peppercorns

- ¼ cup chopped fresh rosemary leaves

- ¼ cup chopped fresh sage leaves

Directions:

1. To make the herb marinade, put all the ingredients into a blender and pulse until smooth (add 2 tablespoons of water if difficult).

2. Rub the pepper and salt into the meat, add two tablespoons of the herb marinade and rub until the meat is coated with the mixture.

3. Put the meat in a broiler and cook for 3-4 minutes on one side over medium heat or until a brown crust forms, then flip and cook for the same amount of time or until the other side is well browned too.

4. Spread the garlic butter sauce on the steak halfway through the cooking time and let coat.

5. Sauté the mushrooms and onion in a pan over medium heat until they are both soft, add the balsamic glaze, stir and allow to cook for a minute or two.

6.   Add the butter and chopped parsley/basil, stir and cook until butter is fully melted and well incorporated.

7.   Put the sautéed mushrooms and onion mixture at the bottom of a large round plate, top with browned steak, then top with crumbled cheese.

Nutrition:

- Calories: 115

- Fat: 14g

- Carbs: 78g

- Sugars: 9g

- Protein: 8g

Ruby Tuesday's Chicken Quesadillas

Preparation Time: 30 minutes

Cooking Time: 45 minutes

Servings: 5

Ingredients:

- 5 ounces chicken bosom

- Italian dressing

- 12-inch flour tortilla margarine

- 1 cup destroyed Monterey jack/cheddar

- 1 tablespoon tomatoes, diced

- 1 tablespoon jalapeno peppers, diced

- Cajun seasoning (to taste)

- ½ cup destroyed lettuce

- ¼ cup diced tomatoes sour cream

Directions:

1. Spot chicken bosom in a bowl with enough Italian dressing to cover; permit to marinate 30 minutes, refrigerated. Barbecue marinated chicken until done in a daintily oiled dish.

Slice to three-quarter, (pieces) then keeps safe. Brush some margarine one side of tortilla and spot in a griddle over medium warmth. On one portion of tortilla, including cheddar, 1 tablespoon tomatoes, peppers, and Cajun preparing in a specific order. Try to spread to the edge of the half. Top with diced chicken, crease void tortilla side on top, and flip over in skillet with the goal that cheddar is on the head of the chicken. Cook until exceptionally warm all through.

2.   Expel from skillet to serving plate and cut into six equivalent wedges on one side of the plate. On the opposite side put lettuce, finished off with ¼ cup tomatoes, and afterward finished off with acrid cream. Serve your preferred salsa in a little bowl as an afterthought.

Nutrition:

- Calories: 242.8

- Fat: 6.6g

- Carbs: 38.4g

- Sugars: 3g

- Protein: 8.4g

Popeye's Red Beans and Rice

Preparation Time: 20 minutes

Cooking Time: 40 minutes

Servings: 10

Ingredients:

- 3 (14-ounce) cans red beans
- ¾ pounds smoked ham hock
- 1¼ cups water
- ½ teaspoon onion powder
- ½ teaspoon garlic salt
- ¼ teaspoon red pepper flakes
- ½ teaspoon salt
- 3 tablespoons lard
- Steamed long-grain rice

Directions:

1. Add 2 canned red beans, ham hock, and water to a pot. Cook on medium heat and let simmer for about 1 hour.

2. Remove from heat and wait until the meat is cool enough to handle. Then, remove meat from the bone.

3.   In a food processor, add meat, cooked red beans and water mixture, onion powder, garlic salt, red pepper, salt, and lard. Pulse for 4 seconds. You want the beans to be cut and the liquid thickened. Drain remaining 1 can red beans and add to the food processor. Pulse for only 1 or 2 seconds.

4.   Remove ingredients from the food processor and transfer to the pot from earlier. Cook on low heat, stirring frequently until mixture is heated through.

5.   Serve over steamed rice.

Nutrition:

- Calories: 445

- Fat: 12g

- Carbs: 67g

- Sugar: 1g

- Protein: 17g

- Sodium: 670mg

Applebee's Sizzling Steak, Cheese, and Mushrooms Skillet

Preparation Time: 15 minutes

Cooking Time: 1 hour and 35 minutes

Servings: 4

Ingredients:

- 1 head garlic, cut crosswise

- 2 tablespoons olive oil, divided

- Salt and pepper, to taste

- 2 pounds Yukon Gold potatoes

- Water, for boiling

- 2 tablespoons butter

- 1 large yellow onion

- 8 ounces cremini mushrooms

- Salt and pepper to taste

- ½ cup milk

- ¼ cup cream

- 3 tablespoons butter

- 2 ½ pounds 1-inch thick sirloin steak, cut into 4 large pieces

- 8 slices mozzarella cheese

Directions:

1.   Preheat oven to 300°F.

2.   Position garlic on the foil. Pour 1 tablespoon olive oil to the inner sides where the garlic was cut, then wrap foil around garlic.

3.   Bake for 30 minutes. Remove from oven, and squeeze out the garlic from the head. Transfer to a bowl or mortar. Add salt and pepper, then mash together. Set aside.

4.   In a pot, add potatoes. Pour enough water on top to cover potatoes. Bring to a boil. Once boiling, reduce heat to medium. Let it simmer for about 20-25 minutes or until potatoes become tender.

5.   Melt butter on a non-stick pan over medium-low heat. Add onions and sauté for about 15 minutes until a bit tender. Toss in mushrooms and sauté, adjusting heat to medium. Season with salt and pepper. Cook for 10 minutes more. Set aside and keep warm.

6.   Drain potatoes, then mash using an electric mixer on low speed. While mashing, gradually pour in milk, cream, butter, and mashed garlic with olive oil. Keep blending until everything is cream-like and smooth. Remove from the mixer and place a cover on top of the bowl. Set aside and keep warm.

7.   Evenly coat steak pieces with remaining 1 tablespoon olive oil on all sides. Heat grill, then place the meat on the grill. Cook for 4 minutes. Flip and add mozzarella slices on top. Cook for another 4 minutes for medium-rare. Add additional minutes for increased doneness.

8.   Transfer steaks to serving plates then top with onion/mushroom mixture. Place mashed potatoes on the side. Serve.

Nutrition:

- Calories: 1159
- Fat: 60g
- Carbs: 47g
- Sugar: 4 g
- Protein: 107g

- Sodium: 1495mg

SIDES & APPETIZER

Stakehouse'sFried Mac and Cheese Balls

Preparation Time: 3 hours and 5 minutes

Cooking Time: 15 minutes

Serving: 4–6

Ingredients:

Sauce:

- 1 ¾ cups marinara sauce

- 1 ¾ cups Alfredo Sauce

- ¼ cup heavy whipping cream

- 1 teaspoon garlic powder

- ½ cup ricotta cheese

- 1 cup Italian blend shredded Cheese

- ¼ cup red wine

Balls:

- 16 ounces grated white sharp cheddar, grated

- 16 ounces smoked gouda cheese, grated

- 3 tablespoons butter

- 2 tablespoons flour

- 2 cups whole milk, warmed

- 1 pound large elbow macaroni, cooked

- Salt and pepper, to taste

- 3 eggs

- 3 tablespoons milk

- 3 cups panko bread crumbs

- Fresh Parmesan cheese for garnish only

- Vegetable oil for frying

Directions:

1. Make the balls. In a mixing bowl, combine the shredded cheddar and shredded Gouda.

2. In a large saucepan, melt the butter. Add the flour slowly, whisking until there are no lumps. Gradually add the 2 cups warm milk. Whisk until smooth, and continue cooking until the sauce begins to thicken.

3. Wait until the sauce has thickened and take it off from the heat and gradually mix in the cheddar and Gouda cheeses and stir well.

4. Add the cooked macaroni and salt and pepper into the cheese sauce and stir well.

5.   Butter a large cake pan spread the mac and cheese mixture evenly into the pan, put in the refrigerator for at least two hours. You want the mixture to set and make it easier to form into balls.

6.   After 2 hours, get the tray from the refrigerator and form the mac and Cheese into evenly sized balls about 2 inches in diameter. Cover, and put them in the freezer for at least an hour.

7.   Beat the eggs and 3 tablespoons of milk together.

8.   Place the bread crumbs in a shallow dish.

9.   Heat enough vegetable oil so that the balls will be covered when you fry them.

10.   When the oil is heated to 350°F, dip each ball in the egg mixture, then the panko crumbs, and drop them into the oil. Work in batches, and cook until the balls are a nice golden brown color, about 3–4 minutes. Transfer to the paper towel as they finish cooking to drain.

11.   Make your cheese sauce by combining the marinara and Alfredo sauce in a small saucepan. Heat over medium and

when warm, add the ricotta, Italian cheese blend, and wine. Stir to combine.

12.   When the cheeses have melted, remove the pot from the heat and add the garlic powder and heavy cream. Stir well.

13.   Serve the macaroni balls with the cheese sauce and a sprinkle of Parmesan.

Nutrition:

- Calories 115

- Fat: 14g

- Carbs: 78g

- Sugars: 9g

- Protein: 8g

ChikFil-A's Raspberry Lemonade

Preparation Time: 2 minutes

Cooking Time: 3 minutes

Serving: 8

Ingredients:

- 1 cup water

- 1 cup sugar

- 1 cup freshly squeezed lemon juice

- 1 ½ cups fresh raspberries

- Added sugar for the rim of your glass

Directions:

1.   In a small saucepan, heat the water and sugar until the sugar completely dissolves.

2.   Meanwhile, purée the raspberries in a blender. Add the contents of the saucepan and the cup lemon juice.

3.   Soaked the rim of your glass and dip it into a bit of sugar to coat the side before pouring the lemonade into the glass.

4.   Serve.

Nutrition:

- Calories: 112

- Fat: 17

- Carbs: 50g

- Sugars: 5g

- Protein: 7g

Olive Garden's Lasagna Fritta

Preparation Time: 20 minutes

Cooking Time: 4 minutes

Serving: 14

Ingredients:

- ⅔ + ¼ cup milk (divided)
- 1 cup grated parmesan cheese, plus some more for serving
- ¾ cup feta cheese
- ¼ teaspoon white pepper
- 1 tablespoon butter
- 7 lasagna noodles
- 1 egg
- Breadcrumbs
- Oil for frying
- 2 tablespoons marinara sauce
- Alfredo Sauce, for serving

Directions:

1.   Place the butter, white pepper, ⅔ cup milk, parmesan, and feta cheese in a pot. Stir and boil.

2.   Prepare lasagna noodles according to instructions on the package.

3.   Spread a thin layer of the cheese and milk mixture on each noodle. Fold into 2-inch pieces and place something substantial on top to keep them folded. Place in the freezer for at least 1 hour, then cut each noodle in half lengthwise.

4.   In a small bowl, mix the ¼ cup milk and egg in another bowl, place breadcrumbs.

5.   Dip each piece into the egg wash then the breadcrumbs. Fry the noodles at 350°F for 4 minutes.

6.   Serve by spreading some alfredo sauce at the bottom of the plate, placing the lasagna on top, and then drizzling with marinara sauce. Put some grated parmesan cheese on top.

Nutrition:

- Calories: 103

- Fat: 21g

- Sodium: 1590mg

- Total Carbohydrate: 82g

- Protein: 9g

PF Chang's Shrimp Dumplings

Preparation Time: 20 minutes

Cooking Time: 10 minutes

Serving: 4–6

Ingredients:

- 1 pound medium shrimp, peeled, deveined, washed and dried, divided

- 2 tablespoons carrot, finely minced

- 2 tablespoons green onion, finely minced

- 1 teaspoon ginger, freshly minced

- 2 tablespoons oyster sauce

- ¼ teaspoon sesame oil

- 1 package wonton wrappers

- Sauce

- 1 cup soy sauce

- 2 tablespoons white vinegar

- ½ teaspoon chili paste

- 2 tablespoons granulated sugar

- ½ teaspoon ginger, freshly minced

- Sesame oil to taste

- 1 cup water

- 1 tablespoon cilantro leaves

Directions:

1. Finely mince ½ pound of the shrimp.

2. Dice the other ½ pound of shrimp.

3. In a mixing bowl, combine both the minced and diced shrimp with the remaining ingredients.

4. Spoon about 1 teaspoon of the mixture into each wonton wrapper and wet the edges of the wrapper, then fold up and seal tightly.

5. Cover and refrigerate for an hour.

6. In a medium bowl, put all together with the ingredients for the sauce and stir until well combined.

7. When ready to serve, boil water in a saucepan and cover it with a steamer. Put a light oil on the steamer to keep the dumplings from sticking. Steam the dumplings for 7–10 minutes.

8. Serve with sauce.

Nutrition:

- Calories: 137.1

- Sodium: 1801.5mg

- Total Carbohydrate: 21.1g

- Protein: 10.5g

SEAFOOD, POULTRY, & BEEF

Applebee's Mac and Cheese Honey Pepper Chicken

Preparation Time: 30 minutes

Cooking Time: 50 minutes

Servings: 4–6

Ingredients:

- 6 slices thick-cut bacon, cooked and chopped

- Seasoned flour:

- 2 cups all-purpose flour

- 3 tablespoons paprika

- 1 ½ tablespoons kosher salt

- 1 ½ tablespoons dry mustard

- 1 ½ tablespoons garlic powder

- 1 ½ tablespoons onion powder

- 1 tablespoon seasoned salt

- ¾ tablespoon black pepper

- ½ tablespoon celery seed

- ½ teaspoon dried ginger

- ½ teaspoon dried thyme

- ½ teaspoon dried basil

- ½ teaspoon dried oregano

- Fried chicken:

- 1 pound chicken tenders

- 2 cups buttermilk

- 2–3 cups oil for frying

- Honey pepper sauce:

- ¾ cup honey

- ¼ cup brown sugar

- ¼ cup pineapple juice

- 3 tablespoons apple cider vinegar

- 3 tablespoons soy sauce

- Juice of 1 lemon

- 1 teaspoon black pepper

- ¼ teaspoon cayenne pepper (or to taste)

- 4 cheese sauce and pasta:

- ¼ cup butter

- 3 cloves garlic, minced

- 1 jalapeño pepper, diced

- 3 tablespoons all-purpose flour

- 2 cups heavy cream

- ½ cup Parmesan cheese, grated

- ¾ cup mozzarella cheese, shredded

- ½ cup Romano cheese, shredded

- ½ cup asiago cheese, shredded

- ½ teaspoon dried basil

- Black pepper to taste

- Fresh parsley for garnish

- 1 pound cavatappi pasta, uncooked (or other short cut pasta)

- 2 tablespoons olive oil, for drizzling

Directions:

1. Mix the chicken in a bowl together with the buttermilk. Rotate the chicken in the bowl to make sure each piece is covered.

2. In a large re-sealable bag, combine all the ingredients for the seasoned flour and shake it up.

3. Combine all the ingredients for the honey pepper sauce. Bring it to a boil over medium-high heat, and then reduce the

heat to low and let it simmer until the sauce thickens. Remove it from the heat.

4.　　Remove the chicken from the buttermilk, then place them in the bag with the seasoned flour and shake to coat. Set them on a baking tray while you coat the remaining pieces. Repeat until all the chicken has been coated with the seasoned flour.

5.　　Put the oil in a skillet in medium heat. Cook the tenders in the hot oil until they are golden brown and cooked through completely. Set aside.

6.　　After that, cook the pasta in a pot of boiling water until it is al dente. Drain and put some olive oil to keep it from sticking together. Cover.

7.　　Melt the butter in a medium saucepan over medium to medium-low heat. Add the garlic and diced pepper and sauté until the garlic is fragrant. Add the flour and whisk to combine. Cook till it turns brown.

8.　　Gradually add in the heavy cream, whisking constantly. Allow it to cook for 5 minutes, whisking the entire time. The cream should thicken and will coat your spoon.

9. Gradually stir in your cheeses until they are completely melted. Stir in the basil and pepper.

10. Mix the pasta to the cheese sauce and combine well to make sure it is all coated.

11. Plate some of the mac and cheese on a serving plate.

12. Coat the chicken tenders in the honey pepper sauce and lay them on top of the mac and cheese.

13. Serve, and enjoy!

Nutrition:

- Calories 150

- Fat 4.2g

- Carbs 40g

- Sugars 1g

- Protein 9g

Red Lobster's Shrimp Gazpacho

Preparation Time: 2 hours

Cooking Time: 0 minutes

Servings: 4–6

Ingredients:

- 20 ounces V-8 vegetable/tomato/bloody mary mix

- 1 tablespoon olive oil

- ½ teaspoons worcestershire sauce

- 2 tablespoon red wine vinegar

- 1 teaspoons fresh cilantro & parsley

- ¼ teaspoons tabasco sauce

- 1 tablespoonl juice

- 1 cup fresh tomatoes

- ½ cup Seeded cucumber

- ¼ cup Celery

- ¼ cup green onions

- ¼ cup bell pepper

- Salt and black pepper

- 1 cup freshly cooked shrimp

To serve: 1 lime

Directions:

1.   Devein and cook the shrimp. Pop it in the fridge to chill.

2.   Prep the veggies. Chop the cilantro and parsley. Slice the onions and into ¼-inch pieces. Dice the bell pepper, cucumber, tomatoes, and celery into ¼-inch chunks.

3.   Combine all of the fixings (omit the shrimp). Chill it for two hours.

4.   Portion into serving dishes and top with two tablespoons of shrimp and a wedge of lime.

Nutrition:

- Calories: 147

- Fat: 17g

- Carbs: 87g

- Sugars: 15g

- Protein: 14g

Cracker Barrel's Campfire Chicken

Preparation Time: 10 minutes

Cooking Time: 45 minutes

Servings: 4

Ingredients:

- 1 tablespoon paprika

- 2 teaspoons onion powder

- 2 teaspoons salt

- 1 teaspoon garlic powder

- 1 teaspoon dried rosemary

- 1 teaspoon black pepper

- 1 teaspoon dried oregano

- 1 whole chicken, quartered

- 2 carrots, cut into thirds

- 3 red skin potatoes, halved

- 1 ear of corn, quartered

- 1 tablespoon olive oil

- 1 tablespoon butter

- 5 sprigs fresh thyme

Directions:

1. Preheat the oven to 400°F.

2. Mix the paprika, onion powder, salt, garlic powder, rosemary, pepper, and oregano.

3. Add the chicken quarters and 1 tablespoon of the spice mix to a large plastic freezer bag. Cover and put inside the refrigerator for at least 1 hour.

4. Add the corn, carrots, and potatoes to a large bowl. Drizzle with the olive oil and remaining spice mix. Stir or toss to coat.

5. Preheat a large skillet over high heat. Add some oil, and when it is hot, add the chicken pieces and cook until golden brown.

6. Prepare 4 pieces of aluminum foil and add some carrots, potatoes, corn, and a chicken quarter to each. Top with some butter and thyme.

7. Fold the foil in and make pouches by sealing the edges tightly.

8. Bake for 45 minutes.

Nutrition:

- Calories: 140

- Fat: 8g

- Carbs: 30

- Sugars: 10g

- Protein: 25g

Cracker Barrel's Creamy Chicken and Rice

Preparation Time: 10 minutes

Cooking Time: 45 minutes

Servings: 4

Ingredients:

- Salt and pepper to taste

- 2 cups cooked rice

- 1 diced onion

- 1 can cream of mushroom soup

- 1 packet chicken gravy

- 1½ pounds chicken breasts, cut into strips

Directions:

1. Preheat the oven to 350°F.

2. Cook the rice. When it is just about finished, toss in the diced onion so that it cooks too.

3. Spray the baking dish with some nonstick cooking spray.

4.   Dump the rice into the prepared baking dish. Layer the chicken strips on top. Pour the cream of mushroom soup on the chicken.

5.   Whisk the chicken gravy with 1 cup water, making sure to get all the lumps out. Pour the mixture on top of the casserole.

6.   Cover with foil and transfer to the oven and let it bake for 45 minutes or until the chicken is completely cooked.

Nutrition:

- Calories: 160

- Fat: 10g

- Carbs: 50g

- Sugars: 6g

- Protein: 12g

Red Lobster's Shrimp Kabobs

Preparation Time: 5 minutes

Cooking Time: 15 minutes

Servings: 8

Ingredients:

- 1 lb. Uncooked shrimp
- 3 tablespoon olive oil
- 3 cloves crushed garlic
- ½ cup dry bread crumbs
- ½ teaspoons seafood seasoning
- Seafood cocktail sauce
- Also Needed: Metal or wooden skewers

Directions:

1. In a shallow mixing container, mix the oil and garlic. Wait for 30 minutes for the flavors to blend.

2. In another mixing container, combine the breadcrumbs and seafood seasoning.

3. Dredge the shrimp through the oil mixture, then coat it using the crumb mixture.

4.   Thread the shrimp onto the skewers.

5.   Grill the kabobs with the top on the cooker, using medium heat for two to three minutes or until the shrimp turns light pink.

6.   Serve with seafood sauce.

Nutrition:

- Calories: 158

- Fat: 10g

- Carbs: 71g

- Sugars: 10g

- Protein: 16g

Cracker Barrel's Sunday Chicken

Preparation Time: 10 minutes

Cooking Time: 10 minutes

Servings: 4

Ingredients:

*   Oil for frying

*   4 boneless, skinless chicken breasts

*   1 cups all-purpose flour

*   1 cup bread crumbs

*   2 teaspoons salt

*   2 teaspoons black pepper

*   1 cup buttermilk

*   ½ cup water

Directions:

1. Add 3–4 inches of oil to a large pot or a deep fryer and preheat to 350°F.

2.   Mix the flour, breadcrumbs, salt, and pepper in a shallow dish. To a separate shallow dish, add the buttermilk and water; stir.

3.   Pound the chicken breasts to a consistent size. Let it dry paper towel and season with salt and pepper.

4.   Dip the seasoned breasts in the flour mixture, then the buttermilk mixture, then back into the flour.

5.   Put the breaded chicken to the pan and fry for about 8 minutes. Turn the chicken as necessary so that it cooks evenly on both sides.

6.   Remove the chicken to either a wire rack or a plate lined with paper towels to drain.

7.   Serve with mashed potatoes or whatever sides you love.

Nutrition:

- Calories: 150

- Fat: 20g

- Carbs: 50g

- Sugars: 9g

- Protein: 15g

Panda Express's Beijing Beef

Preparation Time: 20 minutes

Cooking Time: 15 minutes

Servings: 4

Ingredients:

- 1 pound flank steak
- 1 cup canola oil
- 4 cloves garlic, minced
- 1 yellow onion
- 1 red bell pepper
- 2 tablespoons + 1 teaspoon cornstarch, divided
- ¼ teaspoon salt
- 3 egg whites, beaten
- ½ cup water
- ¼ cup sugar
- 3 tablespoons ketchup
- 6 tablespoons hoisin sauce
- 1 tablespoon soy sauce
- 2 teaspoons oyster sauce

- 4 teaspoons sweet chili sauce

- 1 teaspoon crushed red peppers

- 2 tablespoons apple cider vinegar

Directions:

1. Cut the beef into ¼-inch slices. Place the beef, egg, salt, and 1 teaspoon of cornstarch in a mixing bowl. Refrigerate for at least an hour.

2. In a separate bowl, combine together the water, sugar, ketchup, hoisin sauce, soy sauce, oyster sauce, chili sauce, crushed red pepper and apple cider vinegar.

3. Remove the beef from the refrigerator and place it in a separate dish. Discard the remaining marinade. Sprinkle the beef with 2 tablespoons of cornstarch and stir. Shake off any excess cornstarch.

4. In a medium saucepan, heat the oil over medium-high heat. When hot, fry the beef in batches, about 2–3 minutes. Remove from oil and set on a paper-towel-lined plate to drain.

5. To a large skillet, add 2 tablespoons of the same oil you fried the beef in. Heat over medium-high heat. Add the onion and pepper and let it cook for about 3 minutes.

6.   Add the garlic and cook about 30 seconds more, then remove from the skillet and add to the plate with the beef.

7.   Pour the sauce you prepared to the skillet and cook over high heat until it thickens. Add the beef and vegetables, stirring to coat.

Nutrition:

- Calories: 160

- Fat: 10g

- Carbs: 50g

- Sugars: 6g

- Protein: 12g

Red Lobster's Easy Garlic Shrimp Scampi

Preparation Time: 10 minutes

Cooking Time: 15 minutes

Servings: 4

Ingredients:

- 1 lb. Jumbo shrimp

- 1 teaspoons McCormick's Montreal Chicken Seasoning

- Black pepper & salt

- 1 teaspoons olive oil

- 3 garlic clove

- 3 tablespoon butter, microwaved for 15 seconds to soften

- 1/ cup lemon juice

- 1 cup low-sugar dry white wine

Optional: 1 teaspoons Red pepper flakes

- ¼ cup freshly grated parmesan cheese

- 1 teaspoons Italian seasoning

For the Garnish: Chopped parsley

Directions:

• Peel and devein the shrimp. Give it a good shake of salt, pepper, and chicken seasoning to your liking.

• Add the oil and warm a skillet using the med-high temperature setting.

• Toss the shrimp into the pan for three to four minutes. Once it turns pink, set it aside for now.

• Mince and toss in the garlic to sauté until it is fragrant (1-2 min.)

• Add and simmer the lemon juice, wine, Italian Seasoning, and pepper flakes (1-2 min). Set to low for two more minutes.

• Add the butter to the skillet and toss the shrimp back into the pan. Simmer for one to two minutes, and serve using parsley and parmesan cheese.

Nutrition:

• Calories: 184

• Fat: 4g

- Carbs: 57g

- Sugars: 9g

- Protein: 12g

Applebee's Chicken Cavatappi

Preparation Time: 20 minutes

Cooking Time: 25 minutes

Servings: 5

Ingredients:

- 2 boneless skinless chicken breasts

- ½ cup Italian salad dressing

- 4 Roma tomatoes, seeded and diced

- ¼ cup chopped fresh basil

- 2 tablespoons olive oil

- ¼ teaspoon kosher salt

- ¼ teaspoon pepper

- 1 pound cavatappi pasta

- ½ cup unsalted butter

- 4 cloves garlic, crushed

- 2 cups heavy cream

- ½ cup mozzarella cheese, shredded

- ½ cup Parmesan cheese, grated

- ½ cup Asiago cheese, shredded

- 4 ounces mascarpone cheese

- ¼ teaspoon kosher salt

- ¼ teaspoon pepper

- ½ teaspoon crushed red pepper flakes

- 2 ounces prosciutto

Directions:

1. Put the chicken in bags that are re-sealable and pour in the Italian dressing. Seal the bag and let them marinade in the refrigerator for at least 1 hour.

2. In a mixing bowl, combine the tomatoes, basil, olive oil, and salt. Stir to combine, then cover and set to the side.

3. Cook the cavatappi in a pot of boiling water until al dente.

4. After your chicken has marinated, heat a skillet over medium-high heat. Melt a little of the butter and brown the chicken breasts for about 5 minutes on each side or until fully cooked. Slice them into thin slices.

5. Let the butter melt in the saucepan and add the garlic and let it cook until fragrant. Put in the heavy cream and let it simmer. Reduce the heat and add all the cheeses. Put some

salt, pepper, and red pepper flakes. Stir constantly until the cheese has melted.

6.   Pour the cheese sauce over the cooked pasta, and stir to coat the pasta.

7.   Crisp up the prosciutto in a small skillet.

8.   Serve by placing some pasta on a plate. Top it with chicken, the tomato mixture, and crispy prosciutto.

Nutrition:

- Calories: 100

- Fat: 3g

- Carbs: 21g

- Sugars: 10g

- Protein: 5g

Chipotle's Honey Balsamic Marinated Chicken

Preparation time: 30 minutes to 4 hours

Cooking time: 20 minutes

Servings: 4

Ingredients:

- 2 lbs. boneless, skinless chicken thighs

- 1 teaspoon olive oil

- ½ teaspoon sea salt

- ¼ teaspoon black pepper

- ½ teaspoon paprika

- ¾ teaspoon onion powder

- For the Marinade:

- 2 tablespoons honey

- 2 tablespoons balsamic vinegar

- 2 tablespoons tomato paste

- 1 teaspoon garlic, minced

Directions:

1.   Add chicken, olive oil, salt, black pepper, paprika, and onion powder to a sealable plastic bag. Seal and toss to coat, covering the chicken with spices and oil; set aside.

2.   Whisk together balsamic vinegar, tomato paste, garlic, and honey.

3.   Divide the marinade in half. Add one half to the bag of chicken and store the other half in a sealed container in the refrigerator.

4.   Put the chicken inside the bag to coat. Refrigerate for 30 minutes to 4 hours.

5.   Preheat a grill to medium-high.

6.   Place the chicken to the grill and cook 7 minutes per side.

7.   During last minute of cooking, brush remaining marinade on top of the chicken thighs. Serve immediately.

Nutrition:

- Calories: 485

- Sugar: 0.5g

- Fat: 18.1g

- Carbs: 11g

- Protein: 66.1g

Chipotle'sClassic Grilled Chicken

Preparation time: 8 – 24 hours

Cooking time: 20 minutes

Servings: 4

Ingredients:

*   2 lbs. boneless, skinless chicken thighs

For the marinade:

*   ¼ cup fresh lime juice

*   2 teaspoon lime zest

*   ¼ cup honey

*   2 tablespoons olive oil

*   1 tablespoon balsamic vinegar

*   ½ teaspoon sea salt

*   ½ teaspoon black pepper

*   2 garlic cloves, minced

*   ¼ teaspoon onion powder

Directions:

1.   Mix the ingredients for marinade in a large bowl; reserve 2 tablespoons of the marinade for grilling.

2.   Add chicken and marinade to a sealable plastic bag and marinate 8 hours or overnight in the refrigerator.

3.   Preheat grill to medium heat and brush lightly with olive oil.

4.   Put the chicken on the grill and cook 8 minutes per side.

5.   Coat the chicken in the marinade in the last few minutes of cooking until it reaches the internal temperature of 165°F.

6.   Place the chicken, tent with foil, and allow resting for 5 minutes.

7.   Serve and enjoy!

Nutrition:

- Calories: 381

- Sugar: 1.1g

- Fat: 20.2g

- Carbs: 4.7g

- Protein: 44.7g.

PASTA, SOUP & VEGETABLES

Mimi's Cafe French Market Onion Soup

Preparation Time: 6 minutes

Cooking Time: 1 hour 40 minutes

Servings: 6

Ingredients:

- 6 tablespoons shredded Parmesan cheese

- 6 slices mozzarella cheese

- 6 slices Swiss cheese

- 6 to 12 slices French bread

- 3 tablespoons Kraft grated Parmesan cheese

- ¼ teaspoon garlic powder

- 1 teaspoon salt

- 3 (14-ounce) cans beef broth

- 3 medium white onions, sliced

- ¼ cup butter

Directions:

1. Melt some butter in pot and sauté the onions in it for about 15 to 20 minutes, until they become transparent (when they begin to brown).

2.   Pour in the beef broth, and add the garlic powder and salt to the existing onions. Boil the mixture and let it simmer uncovered for about 1 hour. Add grated Parmesan cheese within the last 10 minutes of cooking the soup.

3.   When the soup has finished cooking, prepare the oven by preheating it to 350°F in order to toast the baguette slices for 10 to 12 minutes, or until they start to turn brown. When done, take them out and set the oven to broil.

4.   To prepare a serving of soup, take 1 cup soup and pour it into an oven-safe bowl. Place one or two slices toasted baguette on top to float and a slice of Swiss cheese on top of the bread slice. Add a slice of mozzarella and sprinkle 1 tablespoon of shredded Parmesan cheese over top.

5.   Put the bowl of soup on a baking sheet and broil in the oven until the cheese starts to turn brown.

Nutrition:

- Calories: 292

- Fat: 18g

- Carbs: 20g

- Protein: 27g

In "N" Out's Animal Style Fries

Preparation Time: 10 minutes

Cooking Time: 30 minutes

Servings: 6

Ingredients:

- 32 ounces frozen French fries

- 2 cups cheddar cheese, shredded

- 1 large onion, diced

- 2 tablespoons raw sugar

- 2 tablespoons olive oil

- 1 ½ cups mayonnaise

- ¾ cup ketchup

- ¼ cup sweet relish

- 1 ½ teaspoon white sugar

- 1 ½ teaspoon apple cider vinegar

- ½ teaspoon salt

- ½ teaspoon black pepper

Directions:

1.   Let the oven be preheated at 350°F and place the oven grill in the middle position.

2.   Put the fries on a large baking sheet and bake in the oven according to package directions.

3.   Put the olive oil in a non-stick skillet over medium heat. Add the onions and sauté for about 2 minutes until fragrant and soft.

4.   Add raw sugar and continue cooking until the onions caramelize. Remove from heat and set aside.

5.   Add the mayonnaise, ketchup, relish, white sugar, salt, and black pepper to a bowl and mix until well combined. Set aside.

6.   Once the fries are cooked, remove from heat and set the oven to broil.

7.   Sprinkle with the cheddar cheese over the fries and place under the broiler until the cheese melts, about 2-3 minutes.

8.   Add the cheese fries to serving bowls or plates. Add some caramelized onions on top and smother with mayonnaise sauce. Serve immediately.

Nutrition:

- Calories 750

- Total Fat 42 g

- Carbs 54 g

- Protein 19 g

- Sodium 1105 mg

Olive Garden's Vegetarian Soup

Preparation Time: 15 minutes

Cooking Time: 1 hour 20 minutes

Servings: 8

Ingredients:

- 3 tablespoons olive oil

- 1 medium onion, diced

- 1 small zucchini, chopped

- 1 (14-ounce) can Italian-style green beans

- 1 stalk celery, diced

- 4 teaspoons garlic, minced

- 1 quart vegetable broth

- 2 (15-ounce) cans red kidney beans, drained

- 2 (15-ounce) cans great northern beans, drained

- 1 (14-ounce) can diced tomatoes with juice

- ½ cup carrot, shredded

- ½ cup dry red wine (optional)

- ½ cup tomato paste

- 1 teaspoon oregano

- 1 teaspoon basil

- ½ teaspoon onion powder

- ½ teaspoon garlic powder

- ¼ teaspoon thyme

- 1 bay leaf

- 3 cups hot water

- 4 cups fresh spinach

- 1½ cups shell pasta

- Salt and pepper to taste

Directions:

1. Heat olive oil and sauté onion, celery, zucchini and carrots over medium heat.

2. Stir in garlic, green beans, and tomato paste. Then add broth, red wine, hot water, tomatoes, green beans, oregano, basil, onion powder, garlic powder, thyme, and bay leaf.

3. Bring soup to a boil and cover. Let it simmer for 45 minutes. Remove bay leaf.

4. Mix in spinach and pasta. Cook for 30 minutes. Serve.

Nutrition:

- Calories: 199

- Fat: 14g

- Carbs: 20g

- Protein: 31g

Olive Garden's Minestrone Soup

Preparation Time: 7 minutes

Cooking Time: 45 minutes

Servings: 8

Ingredients:

- ½ cup seashell pasta

- 4 cups fresh baby spinach

- 3 cups hot water

- 2 bay leaves

- ¼ teaspoon dried basil

- ½ teaspoon ground black pepper

- 1 ½ teaspoons salt

- 1 ½ teaspoons dried oregano

- 2 tablespoons minced fresh parsley

- ½ cup shredded carrot

- 1 (14-ounce) can diced tomatoes

- 2 (15-ounce) cans red kidney beans, drained

- 4 cups vegetable broth

- 4 teaspoons minced garlic

- ¼ cup minced celery

- ½ cup frozen cut Italian green beans

- ½ cup chopped zucchini

- 1 cup minced white onion

- 3 tablespoons olive oil

Directions:

1. Pour the olive oil in a large saucepan over medium heat. Sauté the green beans, zucchini, onion, garlic, and celery for about 5 minutes, or until the onion starts to turn translucent.

2. Mix the broth in the pot, add the drained beans, carrots, spices, tomatoes, bay leaves, and hot water, and boil them all together. When the soup reaches the boiling point, lower the heat and simmer for 20 more minutes.

3. Add the pasta and spinach leaves and cook for 20 more minutes, then serve.

Nutrition:

- Calories: 262

- Fat: 13g

- Carbs: 16g

- Protein: 25g

Chili's Black Bean

Preparation Time: 5 minutes

Cooking Time: 25 minutes

Servings: 6

Ingredients:

- 2 cans (15.5 ounces each) black beans

- ½ teaspoon sugar

- 1 teaspoon ground cumin

- 1 teaspoon chili powder

- ½ teaspoon garlic powder

- 2 tablespoon red onion, diced finely

- ½ teaspoon fresh cilantro, minced (optional)

- ½ cup water

- Salt and black pepper to taste

- Pico de Gallo and or sour cream for garnish (optional)

Directions:

1. Combine the beans, sugar, cumin, chili powder, garlic, onion, cilantro (if using), and water in a saucepan and mix well.

2.   Over medium-low heat, let the bean mixture simmer for about 20-25 minutes. Season with salt and pepper to taste.

3.   Remove the beans from heat and transfer to serving bowls.

4.   Garnish with Pico de Gallo and/or a dollop of sour cream, if desired.

Nutrition:

- Calories: 143.8

- Total Fat: 0.7g

- Carbs: 25. g

- Protein: 9.5.2g

- Sodium: 5.5mg

Mediterranean's Carbonara Spaghetti

Preparation Time: 15 minutes

Cooking Time: 40 minutes

Servings: 4

Ingredients:

- 10 ounces spaghetti

- 6 yolks

- 5 ounces pork cheek

- Pepper

- 2 ounces roman pecorino

- Salt

Directions:

1.   Cut the pork cheek in ⅓ inches strips. In a pan, cook the pork cheek over medium heat for 10 minutes.

2.   Meanwhile, cook the spaghetti in salted boiling water.

3.   In a bowl beat the yolks, add most of the roman pecorino and some pepper. Mix everything.

4.   When the spaghetti pasta is cooked, drain it and pour it in the pork cheek pan with the heat off.

5.   Add the bowl compound and stir fast; the yolks must not cook.

6.   Serve the spaghetti seasoned with some more cheese.

Nutrition:

•   Calories: 186

•   Protein: 22g

•   Carbohydrate: 38g

•   Fat: 8g

Mediterranean's Bolognese Spaghetti

Preparation Time: 15 minutes

Cooking Time: 30 minutes

Servings: 4

Ingredients:

- 13 ounces whole wheat spaghetti

- 26 ounces minced meat

- 1 onion

- ½ celery

- 1 carrot

- 14 ounces tomato sauce

- 1 cup white dry wine

- Salt and pepper

- Olive oil

Directions:

1. Mince the vegetables and heat some oil in a deep pan.

2. Cook the vegetables in the pan for some minutes, add the meat and break it. Add the white wine and let evaporate.

3.   Add salt, pepper and tomato sauce. Cook for 2 hours over low heat.

Nutrition:

- Calories: 136

- Protein: 17g

- Carbohydrate: 18g

- Fat: 5g

Mediterranean's Garlic, Oil and Hot Pepper Spaghetti

Preparation Time: 15 minutes

Cooking Time: 20 minutes

Servings: 4

Ingredients:

- 13 ounces whole wheat spaghetti

- 6 tablespoon olives

- 1 hot pepper

- 1 garlic clove

- Salt

- Parmesan

Directions:

1. Mince the garlic and the hot pepper. Cook the spaghetti in salted boiling water.

2. Put some of the olive oil in a pan and add the garlic and hot pepper. Cook for some minutes.

3. Once the spaghetti are cooked, drain it and pour it in the pan together with the garlic and hot pepper.

4. Season with some parmesan.

Nutrition:

- Calories: 152

- Protein: 20g

- Carbohydrate: 32g

- Fat: 5g

Hard Rock Café's Homemade Chicken Noodle Soup

Preparation Time: 5 minutes

Cooking Time: 1 hour 10 minutes

Servings: 8

Ingredients:

- 3 cups wide egg noodles, dry

- 1 teaspoon minced fresh parsley

- 1 teaspoon freshly ground black pepper

- 1 teaspoon salt

- 4 cups water

- 4 cups chicken broth

- ½ cup diced celery

- 2 medium carrots, peeled and diced

- 1 cup diced onion

- 1 tablespoon butter

- 2 tablespoons vegetable oil

- 1 pound skinless chicken thigh fillets

- 1 pound skinless chicken breast fillets

- Garnish

- Minced fresh parsley

Directions:

1.   Pour vegetable oil in a pot over medium heat. Sauté the chicken breasts and thighs for about 10 to 15 minutes, or until the chicken gets slightly brown on both sides, and they are cooked through. Take the chicken out of the pot, and place them on a cutting board.

2.   After that, add the butter to the pot, then the celery, carrot, and onion. Sauté the veggies for about 10 minutes, while stirring constantly, until the carrots start to soften.

3.   Slice the chicken into cubes, then add them into the large pot alongside the chicken broth, water, veggies, salt, pepper, and a teaspoon of parsley. Boil them all together, and when the soup reaches a boiling point, lower the heat and let it simmer for 10 more minutes. Combine the noodles to the soup, and continue to simmer for 15 more minutes, until the noodles are soft.

4.   Serve the soup in a bowl with sprinkled minced fresh parsley on top.

Nutrition:

- Calories: 302

- Fat: 21g

- Carbs: 18g

- Protein: 30g

Snack & Desserts

Applebee's Cinnamon Apple Turnover

Preparation Time: 15 minutes

Cooking time: 25 minutes

Servings: 4–6

Ingredients:

- 1 large Granny Smith apple
- ½ teaspoon cornstarch
- ¼ teaspoon cinnamon
- Dash ground nutmeg
- ¼ cup brown sugar
- ¼ cup applesauce
- ¼ teaspoon vanilla extract
- 1 tablespoon butter, melted
- 1 sheet puff pastry, thawed
- Whipped cream

Directions:

1. Preheat the oven to 400°F.

2. Spray the baking sheet with some non-stick cooking spray or using a bit of oil on a paper towel.

3.   In a mixing bowl, mix together the apples, cornstarch, cinnamon, nutmeg, and brown sugar. Stir to make sure the apples are well covered with the spices. Then stir in the applesauce and the vanilla.

4.   Cur the pastries into squares. You should be able to make 4 or 6 depending on how big you want your turnovers to be and how big your pastry is.

5.   Place some of the apple mixture in the center of each square and fold the corners of the pastry up to make a pocket. Pinch the edges together to seal. Then brush a bit of the melted butter over the top to give the turnovers that nice brown color.

6.   Put pastry onto the prepared baking pan and transfer to the preheated oven. Bake 20–25 minutes, or until they become a golden brown in color.

7.   Serve with whipped cream on top or vanilla ice cream.

Nutrition:

- Calories: 235

- Fat: 15.8g

- Carbs: 20. 5g

- Protein: 26g

- Sodium: 109mg

Applebee's Cherry Chocolate Cobbler

Preparation Time: 10 minutes

Cooking time: 45 minutes

Servings: 8

Ingredients:

- 1½ cups all-purpose flour

- ½ cup sugar

- 2 teaspoons baking powder

- ½ teaspoon salt

- ¼ cup butter

- 6 ounces' semisweet chocolate morsels

- ¼ cup milk

- 1 egg, beaten

- 21 ounces' cherry pie filling

- ½ cup finely chopped nuts

Directions:

1. Preheat the oven to 350°F.

2. Mix and combine the flour, sugar, baking powder, salt and butter in a large mixing bowl. Cut the mixture until there are lumps the size of small peas.

3. Melt the chocolate morsels. Let cool for approximately 5 minutes, then add the milk and egg and mix well. Beat into the flour mixture, mixing completely.

4. Spread the pie filling in a 2-quart casserole dish. Randomly drop the chocolate batter over the filling, then sprinkle with nuts.

5. Bake for 40–45 minutes.

6. Serve with vanilla ice cream if desired.

Nutrition:

- Calories: 502

- Fat: 1.8g

- Carbs: 10. 2g

- Protein: 19.0g

- Sodium: 265mg

Taco Bells's AM Crunchwrap

Preparation Time: 10 minutes

Cooking Time: 20 minutes

Servings: 2

Ingredients:

- Flour tortillas (2 large)

- Whisked eggs (3-4) + Milk (1 tablespoon)

- Shredded sharp cheddar cheese (2–4 tablespoon)

- Shredded hash browns (heaping 5 cup)

- Hot sauce - mild - your choice (4 tablespoon)

- Bacon (4 crispy)

- Cooking oil spray

- Taco Bell sauce

Directions:

1.   Lightly spritz a skillet using cooking oil spray and warm using the medium temperature setting.

2.   Whisk and add the eggs, salt, and pepper into a skillet. Whisk until they are fluffy and set them aside.

3.   Warm a skillet and heat the tortillas for about half of a minute. Prepare and close them, placing them in a skillet to cook for about 30 to 40 seconds using the medium temperature setting.

4.   Serve with sauce as desired.

Nutrition:

- Calories: 255

- Carbohydrates: 16g

- Protein: 15g

- Fat: 14g

- Sugars: 2g

Applebee's Chocolate Mousse Dessert Shooter

Preparation Time: 1 hour

Cooking time: 0 minutes

Servings: 8

Ingredients:

- 2 tablespoons butter

- 6 ounces' semi-sweet chocolate chips (1 cup), divided

- 2 eggs

- 1 teaspoon vanilla

- 8 oreo cookies

- ½ cup prepared fudge sauce

- 2 tablespoons sugar

- ½ cup heavy cream

- Canned whipped cream

Directions:

1. Melt the butter and all but 1 tablespoon of the chocolate chips in a double boiler.

2.   When they are melted, stir in the vanilla and remove from the heat.

3.   Whisk in the egg yolks.

4.   Beat the egg whites and pour them into the chocolate mixture.

5.   Beat the sugar and heavy cream in a separate bowl until it forms stiff peaks or is the consistency that you desire. Fold this into the chocolate mixture.

6.   Crush the remaining chocolate chips into small pieces and stir them into the chocolate.

7.   Crush the oreos. (You can either scrape out the cream from the cookies or just crush the entire cookie.)

8.   Put some of the cookie crumbs into the bottom of your cup and pat them down. Layer the chocolate mixture on top. Finish with whipped cream and either more chocolate chips or oreo mixture.

9.   Store in the refrigerator until ready to serve.

Nutrition:

• Calories: 389

• Fat: 11.6g

- Carbs: 25. 2g

- Protein: 39.0g

- Sodium: 222mg

Reese's Peanut Butter Cups

Preparation time: 15 minutes

Cooking time: 2 minutes

Chill time: 6 hours

Servings: 10

Ingredients:

- Salt, pinch

- 1½ cups peanut butter

- 1 cup confectioners' sugar

- 20 ounces milk chocolate chips

Directions:

1.   Take a medium bowl and mix the salt, peanut butter, and sugar until firm.

2.   Place the chocolate chips in a microwave-safe bowl and microwave for 2 minutes to melt.

3.   Grease the muffin tin with oil spray and spoon some of the melted chocolate into each muffin cup.

4.   Take a spoon and draw the chocolate up to the edges of the muffin cups until all sides are coated.

5.   Cool in the refrigerator for few hours.

6.   Once chocolate is solid, spread about 1 teaspoon of peanut butter onto each cup.

7.   Leave space to fill the edges of the cups.

8.   Create the final layer by pouring melted chocolate on top of each muffin cup.

9.   Let sit at room temperature until cool.

10.   Refrigerate for a few hours until firm.

11.   Remove the cups and serve.

Nutrition:

- Calories: 455
- Total Fat: 21.7g
- Carbs: 59 g
- Protein: 9.7g
- Sodium: 384mg

Abuelo's Sangria Roja

Preparation Time: 5 minutes

Cooking Time: 0 minutes

Servings: 5

Ingredients:

- 1-liter sangria wine

- ¾ cup white Zinfandel

- ¼ cup Peach Schnapps

- ½ cup Triple Sec

- 1 cup Sprite

- 1 ½ cups orange soda

- ¼ cup brandy

- ½ cup raspberry puree

- 1-ounce rum

Directions:

1.	Combine all ingredients well and serve over fruits of choice: oranges, lemon, lime, peaches, etc.

Nutrition:

- Calories 115

- Fat 14g

- Carbs 78g

- Sugars 9g

- Protein 8g

Applebee's Triple Chocolate Meltdown

Preparation Time: 1 hour

Cooking time: 30 minutes

Servings: 8

Ingredients:

- 2 cups heavy cream, divided

- 1 cup white chocolate chips

- 1 cup semi-sweet chocolate chips

- 1-pound bittersweet chocolate, chopped

- ½ cup butter, softened

- 6 eggs

- 1 ½ cups sugar

- 1 ½ cups all-purpose flour

- Ice cream, for serving

Directions:

1. Preheat the oven to 400°F.

2.   Prepare 8 ramekins by first coating the inside with butter then sprinkling them with flour so the bottom and sides are covered. Place them on a baking tray.

3.   In a saucepan, bring 1 cup heavy cream to a simmer. Remove it from the heat and add the white chocolate chips, stirring until the chocolate is melted and the mixture is smooth. Let it to cool for about a half an hour, stirring occasionally.

4.   Repeat with the other cup cream and the semi-sweet chocolate chips.

5.   In a double boiler, combine the bittersweet chocolate with the softened butter and stir until the chocolate is melts and becomes smooth and remove the bowl from the heat and allow it to cool for about 10 minutes

6.   In a bowl, beat the eggs and the sugar together for about 2 minutes, or until the mixture is foamy. Fold in the bittersweet chocolate mixture.

7.   Beat in flour half a cup at a time in the blender, being careful not to overmix the batter.

8.   Pour the batter evenly and place the baking tray in oven. Bake for about 18 minutes.

9.   When done, the cakes should have a slight crust but still be soft in the middle. Remove them from oven when they have reached this look. If you cook them too long you won't get the lava cake effect.

10.   Let the ramekins sit on the tray for 2–3 minutes and then invert them onto serving plates.

11.   Drizzle some of both the semi-sweet and white chocolate sauces over the top and serve with a scoop of ice cream.

Nutrition:

- Calories: 421

- Fat: 13g

- Carbs: 22g

- Protein: 24.0g

- Sodium: 311mg

Z'tejas' Spicy Blackberry Fruit Cobbler

Preparation Time: 10 minutes

Cooking Time: 50 minutes

Servings: 6–8

Ingredients:

- 1 ¼ cup divided granulated sugar

- 1 cup all-purpose flour

- 1 ½ teaspoons of baking powder

- ½ teaspoon of salt

- 1 cup whole milk

- ½ cup unsalted butter, melted

- 3 cups fresh blackberries

Directions:

1.   Place the oven stand in the middle position and preheat the oven to 350 degrees. Grease a 9-inch round baking dish with a non-stick spray.

2.   Combine 1 cup sugar, flour, yeast, and salt. Add milk and mix until smooth.

3.   Add melted butter and mix until smooth.

4.   Put the dough into a greased baking dish. Lay the berries on top. Sprinkle ¼ cup sugar on top evenly.

5.   Bake until the edges are golden and crispy, 50–60 minutes.

6.   Serve hot with whipped cream or ice cream, if necessary.

Nutrition:

- Calories: 140

- Fat: 8g

- Carbs:30

- Sugars: 10g

- Protein: 25g

Texas Roadhouse's Deep Fried Pickles

Preparation Time: 10 minutes

Cooking Time: 10 minutes

Servings: 4

Ingredients:

- Vegetable oil

- ¼ cup flour

- 1¼ teaspoons Cajun seasoning

- ¼ teaspoon oregano

- ¼ teaspoon basil

- ⅛ teaspoon pepper

- Salt

- 2 cups dill pickles

- ¼ cup mayonnaise

- 1 tablespoon horseradish

- 1 tablespoon ketchup

Directions:

1. Preheat oil in a large pot at 375°F.

2.   Create the coating by mixing the 1 teaspoon Cajun seasoning, flour, basil, oregano, pepper, and salt.

3.   Dip the pickle slices in flour mixture, then carefully lower into hot oil. Work in batches and deep fry for about 2 minutes or until lightly brown.

4.   Using a slotted spoon, transfer pickles to a plate lined with paper towels to drain.

5.   While pickles drain and cool, add mayonnaise, horseradish, ketchup, and remaining Cajun seasoning in a bowl. Mix well.

6.   Serve immediately with dip on the side.

Nutrition:

- Calories: 296
- Total Fat 28g
- Saturated Fat: 14g
- Carbs: 12g
- Sugar: 4g
- Fibers: 0g
- Protein: 1g

Taco Bells's Dressed Egg Taco

Preparation Time: 10 minutes

Cooking Time: 15 minutes

Servings: 8

Ingredients:

- ⅓ cup black beans

- ⅓ cup Pico de Gallo

- ⅓ cup cubed avocado

- 1 tablespoon Lime juice

- 1 cup frozen, thawed potatoes

- ½ lb. bulk pork sausage

- 6 large eggs

- 2 tablespoon milk

- ½ cup Monterey Jack shredded cheese

- 8 @ 6 inches warmed flour tortillas

- Optional Fixings:

- Pico de Gallo

- Sour cream

- Freshly chopped cilantro

Directions:

1.   Rinse and drain the beans.

2.   Gently mix the avocado, beans, pico de gallo, and lime juice.

3.   Cook the potatoes and crumbled sausage using the medium temperature setting until the sausage is no longer pink (6-8 min.)

4.   Whisk the eggs and milk. Pour them into the skillet, stirring over medium heat until the eggs are thickened, and no liquid egg remains.

5.   Stir in the cheese.

6.   Put a spoonful of the egg mixture into each of the tortillas, and top with the bean mixture. Garnish them to your liking.

Nutrition:

- Calories: 291

- Protein: 13g

- Fat: 16g

- Carbohydrates: 22g

- Sugars: 1g

Popeye's Easy Oatmeal Cream Pies

Preparation Time: 20 minutes

Cooking Time: 10 minutes

Servings: 18

Ingredients:

- ¾ cup butter, softened

- 2 large eggs at room temperature

- 1 packet of spice cake mix (normal size)

- 1 cup fast-cooked oatmeal

- 1 can (16 grams) vanilla icing

Directions:

1. Beat butter and eggs together until well mixed. Mix cake and oatmeal mixture. Although the dough is still quite soft, keep it refrigerated and cover for 2 hours or until it is firm enough to roll.

2. Preheat the oven to 350°. Roll half of the dough onto the full surface of the flour to ¼-inch thickness. Cut at 2-½ Flour. Round cookie cutter. Bake for 8 minutes until finished.

Remove the shelf from the shelf and allow it to cool completely. Repeat the remaining dough.

3.	Sprinkle icing sugar on half of the cookies; add other cookies.

4.	Freezing option: freeze the sandwich biscuits installed in the freezing container, and separate the layers with wax paper. Defrost before serving.

Nutrition:

- Calories: 178

- Fat: 15g

- Carbs: 50g

- Sugars: 8g

- Protein: 9g

Cadbury's Cream Egg

Preparation Time: 15 minutes

Cooking Time: 2 minutes + Chill time: 3 hours 30 minutes

Servings: 6

Ingredients:

- ⅓ cup light corn syrup

- ⅓ cup butter

- 2 teaspoons vanilla

- ⅓ teaspoon salt

- 3½ cups white sugar, ground and sifted

- 3 drops yellow food coloring

- 2 drops red food coloring

- 16 ounces chocolate chips, milk

- 3 teaspoons vegetable shortening

Directions:

1. Take a bowl and combine corn syrup, butter, vanilla, salt and powdered sugar.

2. Mix all the ingredients well with a beater.

3.　　Reserve ⅓ of the mixture in a separate bowl, then add food coloring.

4.　　Chill both portions in the refrigerator for 2 hours.

5.　　Form rolls from the orange filling, about ¾-inch in diameter.

6.　　Wrap the orange rolls with white filling.

7.　　Repeat until all of the mixture is consumed.

8.　　Form in the shape of eggs.

9.　　Let sit in the refrigerator for 1 hour.

10.　　Melt the chocolate chips in the microwave.

11.　　Dip each egg roll in the melted chocolate.

12.　　Cool in the refrigerator for 30 minutes.

13.　　Once solid, serve and enjoy.

Nutrition:

- Calories: 104

- Total Fat 34.8g

- Carbs: 174g

- Protein: 5.9g

- Sodium: 261mg

Taco Bells's Cinnabon Delights

Preparation Time: 15 minutes

Cooking Time: 15 minutes

Servings: 24

Ingredients:

- 24 ounces Pillsbury™ refrigerated cinnamon rolls with icing

- 2 teaspoons Cinnamon

- ¾ cup Granulated sugar

- ¼ cup Butter

- ¼ cup warmed caramel ice cream topping

- ¼ cup Betty Crocker™ Rich & Creamy white frosting

Directions:

1.   Heat the oven at 350° Fahrenheit. Prepare a baking tray using a layer of parchment baking paper. Open the rolls and slice each one into three pieces. Roll each one into a ball.

2.   Melt the butter in the microwave. Whisk the sugar and cinnamon in another bowl.

3.   Roll the dough balls through the butter, then the cinnamon and sugar. Arrange them on the baking tin. Bake them until nicely browned (10min.) and cool for another ten minutes.

4.   Warm the frosting for about ten seconds in the microwave to soften it slightly for piping. Scoop the filling into the piping bag.

5.   Squirt in the frosting into the ball until it puffs. Garnish them using the sauce and serve.

Nutrition:

- Calories: 62.1

- Protein: 0.1 grams

- Fat Content: 2.3 grams

- Carbohydrates: 10.7 grams

- Sugars: 7.8 grams

DRINKS

Dunkin' Donuts Salted Caramel Hot Chocolate

Preparation Time: 5 minutes

Cooking Time: 0 minutes

Servings: 1

Ingredients:

- 2–3 teaspoonfuls cocoa powder (unsweetened)

- 1 cup whole milk

- 1 tablespoon caramel syrup (without sugar)

- 2 tablespoons granulated sugar

- ½ tablespoon vanilla extract

- Whipped cream

For Toppings:

- ½ tablespoon sea salt

Directions:

1. Use a large-sized mug for mixing sea salt, sugar, and cocoa.

2.   Maintain a high heat setting in the microwave to heat the milk.

3.   Remove the hot milk from microwave and mix vanilla extract in it.

4.   Mix the cocoa mixture with the mixture of milk. Stir it to get a smooth mixture.

5.   Use whipped cream for toppings and also use caramel syrup for drizzling on the top.

6.   Sprinkle a pinch of sea salt as per your choice.

7.   Serve the hot beverage and enjoy it.

Nutrition:

- Calories: 360

- Protein: 13g

- Fat: 9g

- Carbs: 66g

- Fiber: 2g

Olive Garden's Green Apple Moscato Sangria

Preparation Time: 10 minutes

Cooking Time: 0 minutes

Servings: 6

Ingredients:

- 8 cups ice

- 750ml moscato

½ a cup each of:

- Orange slices

- Strawberries

- Green apple slices

6 ounces each of:

- Apple puree

- Pineapple juice

Directions:

1. Make a mixture of pineapple juice, apple puree, and chilled moscato in a large-sized pitcher.

2. Stir the mixture well.

3.   Take several ice cubes in a glass and pour the iced beverage in the glass before serving it.

4.   Serve and enjoy it.

5.   If you want to have a fun drink at a festive occasion and yet don't want it to contain too much alcohol, then sangria is the drink for you.

6.   Add some slices fruits such as blueberries, orange, strawberries, and so on.

Nutrition:

- Calories: 210

- Protein: 0g

- Fat: 0g

- Carbs: 35g

- Fiber: 0g

Starbucks' Caramel Apple Spice

Preparation Time: 10 minutes

Cooking Time: 10 minutes

Servings: 1

Ingredients:

- 64 ounces of apple juice (100% pure)

- 2 tablespoons flour

½ each of:

- White sugar

- Brown sugar (packed)

- 5 tablespoons powdered sugar

1 cup each of:

- Whipped cream (heavy)

- Water

½ teaspoons each of:

- Vanilla extract

- Cinnamon

- A couple of dashes cinnamon

For toppings:

- Caramel

Directions:

1.   Set the oven at medium-low heat and steam the apple juice in a large-sized pot. Be careful to avoid boiling.

2.   Take a small-sized pot to mix flour, sugar, and cinnamon in it.

3.   Stir the mixture after adding water.

4.   Set the oven at the medium-low flame and boil the mixture for two minutes.

5.   Heat lightly to make the syrup achieve an appropriate thickness.

6.   Remove the mixture from the oven and leave it to cool down. It will increase the consistency of the mixture. Mix the vanilla extract in the mixture.

7.   Use cinnamon dolce syrup for pouring over the steamed apple juice. Otherwise, you can keep the syrup in the dispenser to mix individually in the glasses.

8.   Apply homemade whipped cream as toppings and drizzle the mixture with caramel toppings.

9.   You can fold in a few cinnamon dashes and vanilla as per your preference.

10.   Serve it immediately and enjoy it.

Nutrition:

- Calories: 210

- Protein: 0g

- Fat: 6g

- Carbs: 40g

- Fiber: 0g

Starbucks' Hazelnut Frappuccino

Preparation Time: 10 minutes

Cooking Time: 0 minutes

Servings: 3

Ingredients:

- ½ cup nutella

- 2 cups vanilla ice cream

- 1 cup whole milk

- 6 ice cubes

- 4 teaspoonfuls espresso powder (instant)

For optional:

- Chocolate curls

Directions:

1. Use a blender for mixing nutella, milk, and espresso powder and cover it to blend completely. Combine ice cubes and blend to make a smooth mixture.

2. Then, mix ice cream and blend the mixture by covering it. Make sure the mixture is smooth.

3. Pour the prepared mixture into glasses.

4. Serve immediately to enjoy it.

5. You can garnish the mixture by using chocolate curls as per your choice.

Nutrition:

- Calories: 474

- Protein: 9g

- Fat: 27g

- Carbs: 55g

- Fiber: 2g

CPSIA information can be obtained
at www.ICGtesting.com
Printed in the USA
BVHW041751070421
604344BV00012B/1169